An Ey
to Perce

North Yorkshire Moors Association
www.north-yorkshire-moors.org.uk
Registered Charity No. 517639

First published by North Yorkshire Moors Association, 2010
Copyright text © Derek Statham

A copy of the British Library Cataloguing in Publication Data
is available from the British Library

ISBN: 978-0-9565779-0-0

Front cover photo by Mike Kipling

Design and editorial: Basement Press, Glaisdale
www.basementpress.com

Printed and bound by Camphill Press, Botton, UK

An Eye to Perceive

Memoirs of a National Park Officer

Derek Statham

In Memory of Cathy

Contents

List of Illustrations and Photos

Foreword

The National Parks of England and Wales have inspired millions of people, giving them healthier, happier and fuller lives. They matter to us out of all proportion to the modest investment of public funds that they represent. Yet there are few firsthand accounts of what it is like to run a National Park. National Park Officers, it seems, are not given to writing memoirs; they are reluctant to talk about the political intrigue that often goes with the job, and of the ups and downs of the struggle to protect these areas and secure for them the resources they need. So when Derek Statham tells how it was to be the National Park Officer of the North York Moors National Park for 20 years, we should study it carefully. For we are given a fascinating insight into the never-ending struggle to keep the National Park ideal alive. While each Park is different and faces a special set of challenges, anyone familiar with the Park world will recognise in Derek's account the pressures brought to bear upon the Parks by powerful interest groups – just because these places are beautiful, they are not immune to some ugly forces. The Parks need courageous champions, and nowhere is that quality more important than in the National Park Officer.

We can learn from this account what else is required to be a successful National Park Officer: clear and consistent commitment to a vision, great patience, negotiating skills and the ability to know how far to push your case and when to settle for a compromise. But if these qualities are as important now as they were when Derek took up his post, the period that he describes was one of great change and much progress.

Before 1974, the Parks (with the sole exceptions of the Peak District and the Lake District) were really rather puny institutions. As this account shows, they were likely to be jumped on by their parent county councils if they tried to flex their muscles, and the resources they could draw on were derisory. They were no match for the forces that beset them. But the deal – described by Derek Statham – which was made between the Countryside Commission and the County Councils, and which came into force in 1974, created a single point of administration for each Park and, crucially, brought into being the post of National Park Officer.

It was a hugely important moment in the Park's history. Though some local authority constraints lasted until 1995, when all the National Parks became truly independent bodies, after 1974 they began to take off. It was 'a fresh start' as Derek called it. Supported by changes in public opinion, which was increasingly sympathetic to environmental concerns, the National Parks began, bit by bit, to reverse the long story of decline and retreat that had affected them all in earlier years. It was not plain sailing, of course, and the conflict with agriculture was especially difficult as it often involved individuals who served as members of the Park authorities. Derek's account of how the attitudes among farmers changed is particularly interesting: gradually, farmers and the Parks found more and more common ground, especially after the high water of agricultural production was passed in the late 1980s, the pressure to plough up moorland eased and agri-environmental grants came on stream. The Parks were sometimes the catalysts in finding new ways to bring farming and conservation together, as in the Farm Conservation Plans scheme pioneered by the North York Moors and for whose success Derek Statham is entitled to take much credit.

While landscape and nature make the Parks special places, this is of little social value unless they can also be enjoyed. So access, recreation and enjoyment form the Parks' second purpose. This account covers many aspects, from steam railways to long distance routes for walkers. It is good to see a robust view taken of the rather exaggerated fears of erosion caused by walkers – small beer beside the blot of the Fylingdales Early Warning

Station upon the landscape, for example, and a danger that was sometimes invoked by interests that were more concerned with maintaining privilege than heather cover.

Reading this history reminded me again of how effective the Parks can be at their best, when they become rural development enablers, committed to landscape and nature conservation, promoting environmental protection and working for the interests of both visitors and residents. If you want to see what the jargon phrases 'triple bottom line' or 'sustainability' mean in practice, you can do so in many of our National Parks. It is the success of this approach that justifies the UK National Parks' claim to be among the leaders in terms of Protected Landscapes, or Category V Protected Areas in the system devised by IUCN (the International Union for Conservation of Nature). Though now challenged by IUCN to up their game in terms of nature conservation, the Parks can offer a model of how rural areas should be managed in the longer term and in the broader public interest.

One other more personal reflection. I welcome Derek's generous recognition of the work that the Countryside Commission did for, and with, the National Parks over the time that he was National Park Officer. I am sure that the Parks benefited from having a national voice in the Commission, a body that was also ready to initiate, fund and support innovative ways of managing these special areas. It is right that local people should have a big say in how their Parks are run, but it is unrealistic to expect them to be fully committed to the national purposes as well as meeting local concerns. It is this national conscience that the Commission sought to bring to its relationship with the Parks. It is good to be able to recall now, nearly 20 years later, that I found in Derek Statham someone who was always ready to listen to that message from the Commission. I had great respect for him then and, having read this honest and illuminating account of his time at the helm, I have even greater admiration for his achievements now.

Adrian Phillips
(Director General of the Countryside Commission, 1981–92)

Acknowledgements

The incentive to publish these memoirs came about as a result of a combination of two events. The first was a discussion with Jill Renney of the National Park staff of the North York Moors, who was researching material for a display on the history of the National Park. This prompted me to recall the series of articles I had written on my National Park experience and which had been published in the *Voice of the Moors* in 1997 and 1998. The second was the drawing up of a programme of events and projects for the 25th anniversary of the North Yorkshire Moors Association in 2010.

I am grateful to the Association for publishing the book and particularly for the help and support of the Chairman, Tom Chadwick, and Council member, Albert Elliot.

The North York Moors Authority very kindly offered financial support and I have received much valuable help from Andy Wilson's staff, especially from Jill Renney and Gill Sunley who have assisted with the printing process and provided some of the photographs. Mike Kipling has generously agreed for some of his splendid photos to be included.

The foreword has been contributed by Adrian Phillips, a long-standing friend and colleague and a Vice-President of the Campaign for National Parks.

I would also like to thank the many staff and volunteers, past and present, of the North York Moors who have been such an inspiration and help to me over the years.

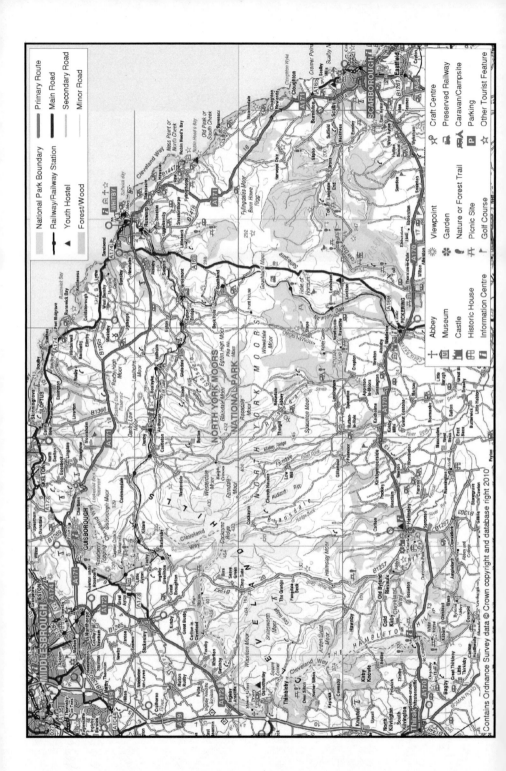

Contains Ordnance Survey data © Crown copyright and database right 2010

Introduction

I FIRST PENNED THESE NOTES about my work as a National Park Officer in the Newsletters of the North Yorkshire Moors Association, *The Voice of The Moors*, in 1997 under the title of 'Moors Management – The Inside Story'. They are here brought together and updated as part of the Association's celebration of its 25th year of work in helping to protect the magnificent landscape of the North York Moors.

The romantic poet Wordsworth, who was a great lover of the Lake District, wrote in the year 1810: '*The Lake District should be regarded as a sort of national property, in which every man has a right and interest who has an eye to perceive and a heart to enjoy*'. It was nearly a century and a half later before his vision was realised in Britain.

I was fortunate enough to be in the driving seat for some 30 years, from 1965 to 1994, when the British National Parks evolved from a group of countryside designations on the Ordnance Survey Maps to distinctive areas highly valued in our National psyche.

A long series of conflicts, accompanied by many discussions and negotiations, was needed to establish this status, which was paralleled by the growth of the conservation movement over this period of time.

The change in attitudes to countryside conservation over 30 years was remarkable and owes much to the pioneering schemes of the National Park teams who achieved the very satisfying objective of harmonising the work of hitherto disparate countryside interests in serving the National Park purposes of conservation and recreation. That this was done sometimes in spite of, rather than because of, government policies makes this achievement even more remarkable.

My working experience extended to both the Yorkshire Parks with some input to the others by way of joint working and discussion, especially with the Broads Authority where, through exchange arrangements, I was able to work in a very different environment.

Trips abroad as a UK representative to EU and other international groups provided much valuable experience though tended to emphasise just how far ahead we were in the type of community-based conservation being practised in our British National Parks. In fact, the British way of protecting valuable but settled and farmed landscapes, like our Town and Country Planning System, has been widely copied and, in effect, become a major export, a point overlooked by most of its critics.

For convenience, the memoirs are divided into four chapters relating to important changes in local and central government organisation or internal staffing changes, all of which affected the work of the National Parks. The views expressed throughout are entirely my own.

Chapter 1

One Man and His Dog
1965-69

I ARRIVED IN Northallerton on New Year's Eve in 1964, fresh from four years as an Area Planning Officer in the fair county of Norfolk. The late night revelry in the street outside my lodgings, combined with the anticipation of a new career, conspired to keep me awake for most of the night. I needn't have worried. I was the first to arrive at the Planning Department in the nearby County Hall at 8.40 a.m. A curious time for offices to open; one of many idiosyncrasies I was to encounter in the old county of the North Riding of Yorkshire, proud of its past and its heritage.

I was taking on the job of National Parks Senior Planning Officer, a sort of general dog's body post set up to provide the day-to-day management of the North York Moors and the North Riding part of the Yorkshire Dales National Park. At least, that was the outline I had received, as job descriptions didn't exist in those days.

The Planning Department was a small, closely-knit unit, but as there was no room for me in the main building, I was given a room in the nearby County Court House. The room was splendid but it was some time before I realised it was required for visiting barristers at the quarterly court sessions and I had to vacate it for periods of about three days. On enquiring of my employers on this matter, it was implied that the best way of dealing with the problem was to take myself off to the National Parks for the duration and catch up on site inspections and visits. I needed little encouragement to adopt this strategy.

Committees

There was only one tier of planning authority in rural areas at that time, the County Council, and so our small department dealt with the whole range of planning control and development plan preparation across the county, in addition to such peripheral matters as National Parks. I later discovered that National Park work had for several years been a weekend task for the County Planning Officer and his Deputy. There was flexibility towards planning work which present-day employers would find remarkable. I was one of only five senior planners and we were expected to tackle any issue or problem that arose in the county, although each had his own specialisation. Thus I soon found my experience of landscape work and development control gained in Norfolk and the West Riding County put to the test.

I also found my responsibilities did not end with the National Park Committees in the North Riding. There was the Joint Advisory Committee for the Yorkshire Dales, which purported to put together the work of the two separate committees for the North and West Ridings, and later the Regional Planning Committee for the North of England, which I was required to advise. Consequently, my initial work was a very mixed bag and included preparing landscape plans for the recently constructed reservoirs in upper Teesdale, siting electricity lines through the Vale of York and organising the annual National Park Authorities Conference, which, that year, was held in the Yorkshire Dales.

On 3 January, my new boss, Sam Lee Vincent, suggested we had a look around the North York Moors. We set off in my new Morris 1100 on a cold sunny day visiting the coast and the Esk Valley and decanting for lunch at the Milburn Arms in Rosedale. Suitably fortified, we faced the Rosedale Chimney Bank, on that day covered by an inch or so of snow. I was unaware of the extreme steepness of the Bank and we only managed to surmount it after much sliding, pushing and cursing! We then proceeded to examine the remains of the old ironstone works at the top of the Bank and to view the extensive range of kilns on the opposite side of the dale. I can clearly remember agreeing that action ought to be taken at some time to prevent the, then already apparent, deterioration in the state of the kilns. Little did I know that it would take some 25 years to achieve this after much decay and crumbling of the structures.

▲
Rosedale Chimney – Demolished in 1972 (National Park Authority – NPA)

Calcining Kilns in Rosedale (NPA)
▼

Struggle

The attitude towards the National Parks at County Hall was curious to say the least. Many councillors regarded the Parks as a sort of socialist 'big brother' that had been thrust on them and resented any expenditure on what they, at best, regarded as luxuries. This attitude was shared to a degree by the senior officers, who thought that the designations unnecessarily complicated the operation of the then relatively new town and country planning system. They felt that the planning system was quite adequate to protect the areas without the need for separate committees. The County Council, which had not supported the establishment of the Parks, had then been given the responsibility for their planning and management. Perhaps only in a democracy like Britain could this sort of thing happen.

I realised early on that I had an uphill struggle to gain some recognition of the value of the areas as National Parks. There was no problem convincing the Council of the need to conserve the landscape; councillors were generally rightly proud and jealous of their heritage. They just could not see why or how National Parks were relevant and they felt threatened by the concept.

Hutton-le-Hole (Mike Kipling)
▼

The prevailing philosophy in the North Riding contrasted markedly with that of the West Riding where, in a totally different political environment, a much more positive and welcoming stance was taken on the designation of the Parks and spending on them. This posed problems for the work of the Joint Advisory Committee for the Yorkshire Dales. The outcome was an unwritten pact not to rock the boat between the two authorities by debating contentious issues or comparing work programmes. The result was a committee which lacked any sort of teeth and usually took the form of a mutual back-scratching session followed by a good lunch in the municipal buildings in Harrogate. By the time of local government reorganisation in 1974, the committee was beginning to develop a worthwhile programme of joint plans and policies, a process aided considerably by an excellent working relationship I had with John Casson, my opposite number in the West Riding.

But going back to the North York Moors and development control, this was a dream compared with my early experience in Norfolk and, I have to say, my later experience in North Yorkshire. There was a tradition of tight control, which few questioned in principle. Area Committees met monthly and went through large numbers of applications at a rate of knots. Occasionally, when the committee could not agree with the recommendation of the planning officer, the application would be referred to the parent committee, which was the National Park Committee if the site was in the Parks, and there would be a full debate.

Under this system, only those proposals which were clearly contrary to approved policy were discussed at length. Planning control had been in force since 1934 in the North Riding, a surprising fact given the conservative nature of the Council. With a healthy attitude towards delegation and the role of officers, a very efficient system had grown up at minimal operational cost. The system lasted until 1974 when, with a two-tier arrangement and more consultation, costs and staffing multiplied.

The results of this long period of control are there for all to see: attractive towns and villages with, on the whole, well-designed buildings and without the intrusive, scattered development so characteristic of rural areas elsewhere. In fact, the chief eyesores in the Moors at the time were wartime remains, then rapidly disappearing, and scattered remnants of mining and quarrying. For example, I well remember the unsightly brick and tile works at Commondale and the Spa Wood ironstone mine at Guisborough, which had just ceased production.

Pressures for Development

The objectives of the National Parks were severely tested during the next few years in the North York Moors. A large reservoir in Farndale, TV masts at Whitby Abbey and Bilsdale West Moor, three potash mines at Boulby, Whitby and Hawsker, extraction of natural gas from the Dalby area and major road improvements through Hutton-le-Hole were just some of the development proposals to confront the Park Committee. Of these, only the Farndale Reservoir, which required legislation, was turned down and then only after a vote in the House of Lords. It represented a rare victory for conservation.

In desperation at the prospect of such an environmental disaster in the centre of the Park, I had begun tentative discussions for another site in lower Rosedale where the landscape, with narrow forested sides, could have absorbed a reservoir with less impact. It was a great relief – if a little disappointing from a purely recreational point of view as the Moors Park has little inland water – that the whole proposal was abandoned in favour of a river abstraction scheme from the River Derwent near York.

It was a time when short-term economic considerations invariably outweighed conservation in these large-scale developments. Indeed, it seemed to me that central government was much less capable than local government at upholding Park principles. And events usually moved at an alarming pace. I can remember being asked to find a site for a natural gas refinery to take the gas from the newly developing field around Dalby and given only three days to come up with a proposal to put to the developing company. I recommended a site in Outgang Lane, Pickering, and was pleased when the suggestion was accepted.

The prevailing attitude towards these important proposals was not to question the need for them or whether the needs could be met in alternative ways but rather to try and ameliorate the impact of them on the landscape. The Bilsdale Mast is a good example of this approach. No one was prepared to challenge the need for better TV reception by using

Upper Farndale – Site of the Proposed Reservoir (NPA)   Bilsdale TV Mast (NPA)

the high ground of the Hambleton Hills; instead the debate was restricted to finding the least damaging site for a mast.

Should the mast and its associated clutter of buildings be erected on the edge of the escarpment, where it would be conspicuous from a wide area outside the Park in the Vale of York, or should it be sited on the back slope where the buildings and associated development could be partly concealed from most views, albeit the mast would intrude more into Bilsdale and the National Park? Eventually, the latter view prevailed and the mast became a dominant feature of the landscape of the Moors.

Interestingly, a similar difficult choice was faced by proposals for a 400 kV electricity line through the Vale of York, with its large pylons. In this case, the alternatives were a line through the centre of the Vale, which would have a major impact on Northallerton and Thirsk as well as presenting problems for aircraft, or a route hard up against the hills where some of the visual impact would be reduced though the line would intrude on views of the edge of the Park. In the end, the second alternative was chosen, the right decision, I feel, but an agonisingly difficult one.

This proposal attracted little public comment and we, in the planning department, were left to negotiate freely. The public and press were, of course, excluded from all Committee meetings in those days. The contrast with the processing of a similar proposal in the late 1990s could not have been more marked with the latter involving public protests, the formation of groups opposing the application, and highly pressurised lobbying of MPs and central and local government personnel.

VIPs

An important body of opinion in all these cases was the National Parks Commission, which became the Countryside Commission in 1968 with a wider remit. Visits from the members and officers of this august body were frequent. There was also a steady stream of senior civil servants and ministers to escort round the Parks, and the frequent changes of government in those days meant a new crop of VIPs to chauffeur around. Donning a peaked cap became a routine, if a little time-wasting, as the turbulent political climate meant that many of those involved were only on the scene for a short period of time.

I can recall many embarrassing and amusing incidents. In 1966, the first, and only, Minister of Natural Resources, Fred Willey, paid a visit to the Moors where he was confronted by a thick sea fret which clung to the whole Park for the day such that he never saw more than about 50 yards into the Park. His local political opponents took much pleasure in this by calling the fret their secret weapon!

The demanding life of ministers was brought home to me on several occasions and my carefully prepared briefs and tours frequently came unstuck. One secretary of state fell asleep in my car near Whitby and didn't wake up until I dropped him off at the station in York. On another occasion, the Chairman of the Countryside Commission actually nodded off during a welcome speech only to be revived later to make a splendid reply, not seemingly having heard a word of what had been said. Later on the same visit, we were all entertained in Mulgrave Woods to the most magnificent picnic lunch I have ever encountered, provided from a huge hamper in the boot of the Rolls-Bentley of George Howard, the Deputy Chair of the Commission.

A frequent visitor to the Moors at this time was the well-known naturalist, James Fisher, who, as a Commissioner, took great interest in the area. He suffered from gout and so our site visits were a bit of a problem though always highly entertaining. A colleague and I virtually had to carry him to the mouth of the cave in Kirkdale, where he was determined to 'sample the atmosphere' of the place enjoyed by the Rev. Buckland who, in the nineteenth century, discovered inter-glacial fossils of tropical animals. He usually brought with him a young friend who was a brilliant naturalist and tested my ornithological knowledge beyond its limits.

Enjoyment of the Park

The management side of the National Park work, as compared with the planning side, was weakly developed and consisted chiefly of finding sites for car parks, loos and picnic areas. Grants for all such schemes were available from the government at the rate of 75 per cent. Staff and day-to-day administrative expenditure were not grant-aided other than Park Wardens and Information Officers, who could receive substantial grants from the Commission. Both the Commission and the government pleaded with us to spend more money on these staff and on projects in the Park, and the grants were freely available.

Car Parking at Sheepwash, Osmotherley (NPA)
▼

Park Ranger with Walkers on the Cleveland Way (NPA)

However, the County Council would have none of it, or only the bare minimum, regarding such expenditure as unnecessary, even frivolous. For these reasons, no information centres or staff were provided in the Moors although a concession was made to appoint a warden after much arm-twisting, partly because it was envisaged that a warden would be able to help landowners with their estate management! The position in the Dales was more favourable, mainly because there were two Committees and two County Authorities involved. Thus a North Riding warden was appointed to match that in the West Riding and, a little later, the latter also appointed an Information Officer to help over the whole Park.

Although spending was minimal, a good deal of scheme preparation at this time led later to some excellent car parking projects at, for instance, Hutton-le-Hole and Sutton Bank in the Moors and Aysgarth Falls in the Dales. The responsibilities for footpath and bridlepath management rested with the Highways Department, where it had a very low priority. Useful liaison arrangements were developed but until the powers were given to Park Committees much later on, very little work was done on the rights of way network. The one bright spot in the Moors was the designation of the Cleveland Way in 1969, the country's second long-distance trail and largely within the Park. Even on this national trail, it was some time before a comprehensive programme of works and improvements was formulated, greatly aided by a generous 100 per cent Commission grant.

The country's first long-distance trail, the Pennine Way, which traverses the Dales Park, had a head start for funds and resources, having been designated in 1965.

Dick Bell was appointed as a warden for the Moors just before I arrived and we immediately struck up a fruitful friendship and dialogue. I enjoyed testing my ideas on him as we walked to inspect a site or a footpath problem. Dick had the countryman's eyes and developed an unrivalled knowledge of the Moors. A similar relationship was evolved with the newly appointed warden for the North Riding Dales, Norman Crossley, who, I recall, had to manage with a bicycle for some time as there was a shortage of Land Rovers.

We all saw the need to take a more positive attitude towards visitors and tourism in general and thought that the Parks would benefit in the long run from enabling visitors to enjoy the resources of the Parks rather than merely viewing the scenery from a car or coach. This may seem old hat, but in the 1960s it was quite new. Undoubtedly, the seeds of National Park visitor management were deeply sown at this time and it was stimulating, as well as challenging, to make a tentative start on such matters as trails and guided walks, aided by a growing band of Voluntary Wardens.

Loss of Moorland

During the 1960s and 1970s, large areas of moorland were lost to forestry and improved farming. No great opposition was mounted to this 'reclamation', as it came to be called. It was regarded as inevitable, the natural order of things, and my task was to attempt to obviate the more intrusive impacts on the character of the area by landscaping, siting fences and contouring forests to avoid harsh lines and skylines.

A shining exception to this sad process was the afforestation of the former Ministry of Defence estate of Newton House near Whitby. With the advice of Dame Sylvia Crowe, a well-known landscape architect, I was able to help

Maybeck in the Newton House Estate (NPA)

the Forestry Commission draw up an integrated land-use and management plan. I was delighted to advise on this scheme, one of the first of its kind, in an unrivalled opportunity to create a new landscape for public enjoyment.

Later, the loss of moorland was to reach epidemic proportions before action was taken to protect it, with, it has to be said, very little help from central government.

By 1968, I had moved up into management as Assistant County Planning Officer but, in a time of staffing shortages the like of which we can only imagine today, I took my Park responsibilities with me. Shortly after this, a new County Planning Officer had been appointed and we moved into an era of expansion of Park work with more resources. The scene was now set for the introduction of new approaches to the management of the countryside.

Chapter 2
County Hall Rules, OK?
1969-74

THE LATE 1960s WAS an exciting time to be engaged in countryside planning and management. The agricultural reforms of the post-war government had been successful in raising food production, though increasingly at the expense of the environment. Afforestation continued apace in the uplands, though with growing unease about the effects of blanket conifers on moor and fell. Improving living standards had led to a virtual explosion of recreational use of the countryside with a rapid growth of traffic. Most visitors did not stray far, however, as the rights of way network, though well placed to accommodate the demand for outdoor exercise, remained undeveloped and, indeed, virtually unknown in many areas.

Heather to Barley

Conflicts were beginning to emerge between competing uses: between farming and wildlife, farming and recreation, forestry and amenity, tourism and local communities.

In the North York Moors, all these trends were evident and there was the additional and important problem of the competition for land between farming, forestry and grouse shooting on the open moors.

▲
Typical Coniferous Forestry (NPA)
On the Moorland Plateau at Kildale Moor (NPA)
▼

Large areas of moorland, particularly in the triangle of land between Whitby, Pickering and Scarborough, disappeared in this period. One of the saddest aspects of this 'reclamation' was that it was heavily subsidised by the public through the Ministry of Agriculture, who encouraged all attempts at food production. The bogey of a national shortage of food was the major driving force behind the subsidies and grants. It continued as late as 1975 with the publication of a policy white paper on 'Food from our own Resources' long after it had become evident that food surpluses, not food shortages, were the coming problem. So the Gilbertian situation of one arm of government in the Ministry of Agriculture paying out large sums of money to destroy valuable habitats and features while another arm through the Department of the Environment tried to stop them was to continue for some years.

The Effects of Moorland Reclamation – Grass Pasture, right; Heather Moor, left (NPA)
▼

The loser was invariably the moorland and some of the changes were quite dramatic in their impact; from heather to barley in one season was commonplace such that an occasional visitor would wonder whether he was returning to the same area. I had many, many difficult negotiations with farmers, usually to little effect as the Park's chequebook was virtually empty. One series of meetings with a farmer, who felt he had a Divine calling to reclaim the wilderness of the moors, would begin with a prayer meeting though it was made quite plain where the Divine sympathies would lie!

Along with other land-use planners, I was to learn, in no uncertain way, of the power and the strength of the agricultural lobby. I remember being taken to task by an irate National Farmers' Union representative who contended that I was hardly in a position to recommend changes to farm businesses as my salary was guaranteed by the public purse. When I pointed out that so was the income of his members and, unlike them, I was publicly accountable for my performance, the discussion got on to a more rational level. On a more positive note, it was undoubtedly the long and patient debates and negotiations which made such a major contribution towards the change in attitudes in conservation in the 1970s, attitudes which we take for granted today.

We were not alone in the North York Moors in facing this problem. On Exmoor, the controversy surrounding moorland reclamation was so great that the government was forced to set up an inquiry, which found decisively in favour of stopping the process and conserving the remaining moorland. This was all dressed up in very reasonable language but there was no denying the inevitable U-turn in policy. At the height of the controversy, I was invited to speak at the AGM of the Exmoor Society who had led the campaign against moorland ploughing. I have never before, nor since, witnessed such passion over countryside affairs, passion so great that no representative of the National Park Authority had been prepared to attend the meeting.

In both the Yorkshire Dales and the Moors, the regrettable practice of moor drainage by 'gripping' or the digging of channels to take away surplus water was common and, again, despite the ecological objections, continued apace with agricultural grants. Ironically, as with hedge removal, the public is now paying to undo the damage, in this instance by blocking the drains to restore wet habitats, which have been shown to greatly benefit moorland flora and fauna.

Comprehensive Countryside Planning

The concern about the deteriorating state of the environment, which had started in the early 1960s with the publication of such polemics as *Silent Spring* by Rachael Carson, now reached the point in the UK where it was obvious that government would have to get its act together and, at the very least, provide a degree of co-ordination and harmonisation between the different users of rural land.

To their credit, the Countryside Commission recognised this need and embarked on a series of experimental studies aimed at across-the-board integration of policies for the competing uses. Two studies in lowland areas in Hampshire and Sherwood Forest were joined by a study of upland problems in the Northern Pennines. I was asked to chair this study, which was carried out by a team drawn from North Riding County Planning Department, the Ministry of Agriculture, the Nature Conservancy Council and the Countryside Commission, with input from other government departments and agencies. It was an exciting challenge to pilot such a prestigious experiment, and a great reflection on the regard held by our small countryside planning team at County Hall.

The results of the study, published in 1974, were inevitably controversial and in many respects well ahead of the time though they were generally well received and made a major contribution to not only the debate on the future of the countryside but also on how to go about preparing comprehensive, across-the-board plans. One of the most controversial features of the study, and one which received much publicity and criticism in the farming press, was a suggestion to create a large experimental wilderness area in the Pennines. The rationale for this was that nature, unhindered by man, would produce over time an environment of great scientific and aesthetic interest. It was hoped to test ideas and perceptions about wildlife, which were somewhat speculative because of the lack of wildness in Britain.

The suggestion was enthusiastically supported by the Nature Conservancy Council and by most other agencies but the idea was so alien to the culture of the farming and landowning community that it stood little chance of success. Indeed, it needed a sympathetic, or at least a benign, landowner who was willing to set aside a large area of land, and, more importantly, to face the opposition of his peers. No such person was forthcoming and the project remained just an eccentric idea until, of course, recent years when a number of schemes with similar aims have emerged. It was, on reflection, decades ahead of its time, although the sort of scheme an early Victorian landowner might have got enthusiastic about. This latter thought depressed me as it was clear that we needed bold and imaginative thinking to break out of the mould of continuing intensification in agriculture.

I clearly recall being taken to task by one aristocratic landowner who thought we were about to ruin his grouse shooting. The prospect, as he saw it, of all those vermin descending from the wilderness was losing him sleep and he obviously thought we were living on another planet.

One of the reasons the Countryside Commission chose the North Riding for the study was without doubt because of the experience, skills and enthusiasm of the county planning team at Northallerton. We had formed a National Park and Countryside section with some very able staff and embarked on an ambitious programme of positive works and experimentation throughout the county but concentrating on the National Parks. It was a great time for young planners to innovate with new ideas for managing the countryside as there was much encouragement from government agencies at both central and local levels.

I had a wide range of responsibilities at this time, including the preparation of one of the first Structure Plans in the UK, covering the area of South Teesside, but I was fortunate enough to be able to take a break from my local government job for a few months. I was seconded to the Centre for Environmental Studies, a government research agency, to study in some depth the background to the land-use conflicts that were building up in the countryside. I was accommodated in the geography department at Durham University and spent a very rewarding few months experimenting with the application of a new technique of Land Potential Analysis to the problems of land use in upland areas, and the moorlands in the Whitby–Pickering area in particular.

This technique and several similar analytical methodologies were fashionable for a time. They became less popular as their objectivity often gave results that were contrary to official policy, and politicians found them hard to swallow, particularly as some of their findings seemed simplistic. This was certainly the case with my Moors studies, which tended to show up forestry in a very favourable light as against grazing and other moorland uses.

Forestry schemes were cropping up in many areas in both the Dales and the Moors. In the Dales, one particularly large scheme in Langstrothdale was refused a forestry grant on environmental grounds, a rare event, though several smaller, but still substantial, projects went ahead in the upper Wensleydale area. Although not welcomed by the Park Authority or the public at large at the time, it has to be said that, with maturity, these woodlands have added to the landscape and, ironically, are now home to a colony of red squirrels, which, alone, is ample justification for their existence. Forestry is a long-term business and requires patience and not a little imagination to judge its impact.

Conserving the Daffodils

Another pioneer scheme in the Moors, in Farndale, promised much but also suffered for being ahead of its time. Conserving the wild daffodils of this Local Nature Reserve had long been a preoccupation of the Park Committee and rumours were rife that the daffodils were declining. I sensed that the time was right for a lasting solution and, after much discussion and negotiation, managed to obtain the support of all the landowners and occupiers in the dale downstream from the proposed reservoir site for a management scheme. This involved fencing off the main areas of daffodils to prevent grazing damage and a programme of maintenance in return for modest annual payments; what we would now call a 'management agreement'.

I put this to the Park Committee for approval with some pride and pleasure as I thought that the involvement of all the farmers and landowners would be sure to achieve a good result. To my surprise and great disappointment, it was voted down on the grounds that paying farmers to conserve wildlife would set a most dangerous precedent. What was even more surprising was that this opposition was led by the appointed members rather than the councillors on the Committee; members who were supposed to take a broader view of countryside matters. Thus ended what would have been perhaps the first modern management agreement.

Farndale Daffodils (Gillian Kent)

The sticking point was one that we would hardly recognise today. One member put it in the following way: 'Farmers are stewards of the land and it is their moral duty to look after the wildlife and the environment, they should not expect the public to pay for it.' How things have changed!

The threat of major development in the Park continued with revised plans for the Farndale Reservoir. Rather than a direct supply scheme for Hull, for which the necessary legislation already existed, a scheme using abstraction from the rivers downstream, boosted by water from the reservoir in times of low rainfall, was preferred. This required fresh legislation. The Park Committee had a very positive debate about the possible recreational uses on it aided by advice from the Regional Sports Council. Attempts to create a major sailing and water sports centre, for which the potential certainly existed, were firmly resisted but all were agreed on some modest provision for water recreation. All these came to nought when the scheme was finally rejected by Parliament.

The protection of the upper dale over several decades for water supply meant that the farms were run down but unspoilt with very little building or intensification of farming. This made it the ideal site for the introduction of the ground-breaking Moors Farm Scheme later on.

Two more potash mines were proposed along the coast and I can remember feeling very depressed that National Park designation seemed to count for so little with these large developments. The policies to protect the Park were in place, but politicians giving greater weight to traditional industries and the promise of jobs nearly always ignored them. I argued that a careful, long-term exploitation of the coastal potash deposits was needed, not a sudden boom which would probably soon burst leaving an even more depressed economic situation with large numbers of workers suddenly unemployed.

Owning Land – Long-term Safeguard

Immediately before the reorganisation of local government in 1974, I began to explore the possibility of the Park Committee purchasing some areas of the Park which were critical in the landscape and that were threatened by agricultural and forestry changes over which the Park Committee had no control. Ownership of the land seemed to be the only safeguard and, although there was much opposition, no one could come up with an alternative that would protect the areas concerned within a reasonable budget. The agricultural grants and subsidies made management agreements so expensive and most moorland owners did not want them in any event.

Thus the Park Committee, through the County Council, eventually became the owner of the Levisham Estate and the Hole of Horcum. Much of the moorland around the Hole of Horcum had already been 'reclaimed' and the only constraint preventing the ploughing of Levisham Moor was its common land status. This was by no means a complete safeguard, however, as a syndicate of farmers from the East Riding were attempting to buy up the common rights as a first stage in a ploughing scheme.

One or two brave souls were resisting the pressures put on them but I was told of one incident which had the trappings of a Wild West tale in

rural England. Apparently a posse of men arrived one Sunday morning at the remote home of one common-right holder and refused to leave until he had signed away his common rights. I do not know the outcome of this particular story but it was all very worrying to those of us bent on conserving the moor with its great scenic, wildlife and archaeological value.

It was with a huge relief when agreement was reached for the County Council to purchase the moor, thus halting the seemingly unstoppable process of moorland reclamation along the corridor of the Whitby to Pickering road.

I was greatly appreciative of some of the senior members of the County Council who were prepared to make a stand for the protection of the moor against the opposition of many other members who viewed purchase as a form of land nationalisation. They included Col. Lawrence Jackson, Chairman of the Park Committee until 1974, Sir Meredith Whittaker, Chairman of the County Councils Association, and Lord Downe, who, with his land-owning experience, did much to calm the fears of members who thought that the ratepayers would be taking on a heavy, long-term burden.

▲
Hole of Horcum (Mike Kipling)

Ironically, the key decisions on this matter rested not with the Park Committee but with Finance Sub-Committees meeting at County Hall. This was a factor in the arguments about the financing and independence of the National Park authorities, which was to emerge later.

Every battle has its loser, however, and I was extremely saddened when later one of our well-respected farming members, Robin Baker, chose to leave the Committee because of its opposition to moorland ploughing.

The Unholy Alliance of Eaton Square

Despite all the time and energy spent on these and other land use issues, local government reorganisation loomed and the Parks were caught up in a fierce controversy over their future governance. Park enthusiasts saw this as an opportunity to gain the longed-for independence while the Counties, much stronger bodies then than their present-day slimmed-down counterparts, were equally determined to hang on to the Parks.

Eventually, a compromise was reached between the two factions: an agreement duly dubbed 'the unholy alliance of Eaton Square' at the offices of the County Councils' Association, where some of the negotiations took place.

This provided the framework for a new system of management for the Parks with a single committee serving multi-county Parks advised by a National Park Officer and a new type of land-use management plan, the National Park Plan, largely based on the experimental studies of the 1960s. Key figures in the process were Reg Hookway, Chief Officer of the Countryside Commission, and Sir Meredith Whittaker, the Chairman of the County Councils' Association, a resident and lover of the Moors.

The unholy alliance brought to an end the management of the Parks by the North Riding Planning Department. The late 1960s and early 1970s had been a very productive period with a small staff constantly innovating and moving on in an atmosphere of growing confidence. The Moors and Dales Parks had benefited greatly from this, though the Dales had been saddled with the two-county split, and a reservoir of skills had been built up which was to form the backbone of the new Park departments.

While most of us directly involved felt that the Parks needed more independence, we were not enamoured with the new, two-tier, system of local government. It seemed to us to have all the right ingredients for a bureaucratic nightmare, and so it later proved. Planning was particularly badly affected. In place of the single-tier, single-staffed county, we now had one county planning department, eight district planning departments and two new National Park departments over roughly the same area. And, worst of all, most of the new authorities went over to a party political system with all the extra bureaucracy and administration that involves.

This meant a job bonanza for the professional staff. I was put into a difficult position as I was eligible for senior posts in all the Yorkshire Planning Authorities, some of which were offering very high salaries, but the new National Park Officer posts were delayed because of disagreements over their terms and duties between the Councils and the Countryside Commission. I was grateful to the new County Council for North Yorkshire which offered me a senior post on the clear understanding that I would be interested in the National Park Officer posts when they were eventually advertised.

In 1974, I was appointed to the post of National Park Officer for the Moors, which I was to occupy for the next 20 years, despite other attractive positions beckoning elsewhere. At my job interview, I picked up one useful lesson for the future. If you want to take the steam out of weighty or controversial issues on a committee agenda, slip in an innocuous item which all can disagree on without losing face. In amongst all the usual questions at my interview was a query about bracken control. My answer provoked a heated debate, which the long-suffering committee members obviously enjoyed after what must have been a tedious day of interviews.

Chapter 3
A Fresh Start
1974¯79

'We trained hard but it seemed that every time we were beginning to form into teams, we would be reorganised. I was to learn later in life that we tend to meet any new situation by reorganising, and a wonderful method it is for creating the illusion of progress while producing confusion, inefficiency and demoralisation.'
Caius Petronius, sometime Roman Consul, *c. AD 400*

A SITUATION OF NEAR chaos reigned in local government in the early months of 1974 as the new system of counties and districts was introduced. The National Parks were caught up in this with the new committees meeting in 'shadow' form to establish their modus operandi while the old committees continued to carry the workload for everyday decision making; all had to be serviced by the same small and daily diminishing staff in the County Planning Department at County Hall.

All Fools' Day, 1 April, seemed a particularly appropriate day on which to usher in a new system of government, hopelessly compromised by a built-in split of responsibilities between the two tiers. The new single-committee arrangement for the National Parks was, in fact, one of the few bright spots in this Balkanisation process. Caius Petronius would have felt at home in Britain in 1974.

Staffing

Our main problem in the early months was the dearth of qualified staff, particularly town and country planners. The recruitment rules restricted appointments in the new authorities to the staff of the existing departments within strictly defined catchment areas in the first instance. This meant that the staff of the North Riding Planning Department could apply to no less than 11 new planning authorities in North Yorkshire, as the new county was to be called, plus the authorities in the new County of Cleveland. As I was not appointed until 1974, many of the qualified staff had already accepted posts in the new departments.

I inherited only four staff from the North Riding County: the Head Warden, Dick Bell, and his assistant, Colin Dilcock; the Information Officer, Ian Sampson, and Field Assistant, Les Sayer, who had been recruited primarily to organise litter clearance in the Park. Fortunately, some of the planners in the old North Riding Department were as determined as I was to continue our work in the National Parks and the newly appointed Yorkshire Dales Officer, Dick Harvey, and I were able to

Danby Lodge – Shortly after Opening (NPA)
▼

rescue some very able officers from the rapidly depleting pool. National Park work clearly had its attractions, despite the relatively low salaries. Thus, I appointed Nick Pennington and Mike Webster as Assistant National Park Officers and we set about finding others to join us.

I was given a fairly free hand in drawing up a new department but added to the problem of the severe scarcity of qualified staff was the lack of funding to pay for them. This was the old percentage problem. The new system of grant aid from central government, which was the main component of our budget, was, in time-honoured, civil service fashion, based on the previous expenditure of the old authority. In the case of the Moors, this had been minimal, even when compared with the Yorkshire Dales, which had benefited from financial inputs from two counties prior to 1974.

Eventually, these problems were overcome though it was some two years before we had even a skeleton-staffing framework. In the meantime, ongoing responsibilities such as development control meant we had to take on part-time and temporary staff. It was an unusual experience to have working for me my previous chief, the North Riding County Planning Officer, Norman Ayling, and the former Whitby Area Planning Officer, George Bell, both of whom rallied to my call for help with the planning applications and deferred their retirement.

This tradition of planning officers helping with whatever task the moment demanded, including serving on National Park Committees, has regretfully disappeared. As was frequently the case in those days, Norman Ayling, on retirement, was appointed to the Yorkshire Dales Committee as a Secretary of State member, where he was able to make a valuable contribution. Such appointments are frowned on these days for reasons of political correctness, which I have never fully understood. What a waste of talent and experience.

In between all the tasks of reorganising and processing the planning applications, we managed to make some progress on projects such as the new visitor centres at Sutton Bank and Danby Lodge. Staff recruitment continued to occupy much of my time, however. Thankfully, the attractions of working in a National Park helped to counterbalance the inferior salaries I was permitted to offer. Some of the staff I recruited at this time remained with the National Park Authority until their retirement, including Stuart Copeland, who took charge of development control, and Val Dilcock, who joined us fresh from college, reflecting the tradition of loyalty to the Park and the job.

Accommodation

Amongst the first list of priorities was the need to establish a Park Headquarters. The County Council wanted the department to stay at County Hall. While this would have certain administrative advantages, I thought it essential for the new authority to be identified with the Park. Life in a Portakabin in Northallerton, remote from the Park and its communities, seemed entirely the wrong environment for young professionals on whose skill the future of the Park depended.

I carried out a quick though fairly exhaustive search for a suitable building in the Park, or close to the boundary, narrowing the choice eventually to redundant council offices in Whitby, Stokesley and Helmsley. With the help of the new Park Committee Chairman, Michael Foster, who lived near Helmsley, an agreement was reached to rent and later to purchase the Old Vicarage there from the District Council who, nevertheless, retained some rooms for a while along with the Forestry Commission. Until such time as we could occupy the whole building, staff were accommodated in temporary accommodation in County Hall, in Kirkbymoorside and later in Danby Lodge.

The Northallerton–Helmsley road, once a moorland road over the Hambleton Hills but rapidly being converted to farming and forestry, became a daily feature in my working life. Its changing moods in summer and winter and the quite amazing variety of weather conditions from end to end provided some compensation for the time spent travelling from meeting to meeting.

I was equally determined that our new Committee should meet in the Park and after much arm-twisting and a building bankruptcy, we were able to construct an extension at the rear of the Old Vicarage which gave us a purpose-built committee room and some much needed office space. After some initial misgivings, the County Council's Officers worked hard to help provide this facility, which absorbed most of our capital for some time.

▲
The Old Vicarage, Hemsley – Park Headquarters since 1974 (NPA)

Looking back, I am sure it was worth the sacrifice of forgoing other capital projects for a couple of years though, unlike later years, very little help was forthcoming in the form of a central government grant to assist us with a 'one-off' expenditure. This and some other decisions involving expenditure attracted a good deal of local opposition in an unfavourable economic climate and it was not a time for the faint-hearted. By 1977, we were able to house all the professional staff at the Old Vicarage and could begin to operate with greater efficiency.

Another priority demanding attention was equally controversial but much more congenial to both officers and Committee members. The North York Moors National Park had, until this time, as its logo the White Rose of York, which it shared with the Yorkshire Dales Park. Both Park Committees decided a new symbol was needed, and in the Moors we chose to hold an open competition to assist the choice of design.

The shortlist came down to a choice between the White Rose, a grouse or a moorland cross. Eventually, after a long debate and by majority voting, the cross of Young Ralph on Blakey Rigg was selected as the centrepiece of the new logo and the final design was worked up by graphic designers in the department. An impassioned speech by Major Peter Walker, then an appointed member of the Committee and later a founder member of the North Yorkshire Moors Association, swayed the decision in favour of a moorland cross.

I must confess to having had reservations about the choice of a cross, instinctively preferring a more animate emblem such as a grouse, but I need not have worried. The cross was an immediate success, being acceptable to most shades of opinion in the very many and diverse groups with an interest in the Park; and so it remains.

▲
The National Park Emblem since 1974 (NPA)

Initial Work Programmes

An early requirement for the new Committee was the preparation of the first National Park Plan, a new concept but one we were peculiarly fitted to undertake with our experience of the experimental land management plans in the old North Riding. I had, in fact, been involved at the national level in securing the place of a management plan in the legislation setting up the new authorities for the Parks. We decided to set a fast pace and prepare the plan as soon as possible, mainly because I felt the need to put the paperwork behind us and get on with much needed projects and management schemes in the Park. We felt we had a good grasp of what was needed in the Park; all that had been lacking was the time and staff to implement the ideas.

It was a time of great debate about the future of land-use policy and there were many opportunities to test new techniques in land management. There was also some catching up to do in sectors of our responsibilities that had been neglected in the past, like the provision of visitor centres and youth education on the environment.

The Amenity Tree Planting Scheme, started in 1975, seems old hat now. At the time, it was one of the first of its kind and was soon joined by a pilot Upland Management Scheme, concentrating on stone wall maintenance and, later, by a Village Improvement Scheme implemented through Parish Councils. This raft of projects and grant aid schemes formed the positive side of our work, along with the provision of visitor facilities, and was to grow rapidly during the next few years.

At this time, another far-reaching development was the transfer of the legal responsibilities for the public rights of way network from the County Council's Highway Committee in North Yorkshire to the National Park Committee. I had campaigned for this change for some time as I felt it was essential for the Park Committee, with the statutory objective of promoting public enjoyment of the Park, to plan and manage the network in combination with all the other management work. Furthermore, it made more effective use of the wardening resources at our disposal. We now had four full-time wardens and a growing and enthusiastic band of volunteers who did much useful work, particularly at weekends.

In this regard, we were ahead of most of the other Parks, who had to contend with footpath management at arm's length. However, the picture was not quite perfect as Cleveland County Council, a very different body from North Yorkshire, would not cede their powers for the small area of the Park around Guisborough, despite the attraction of the Park grants that were available.

The different political and social nature of our parent County Authorities meant that I had to adopt a somewhat Jekyll and Hyde approach in my dealings with them. In extreme terms, this meant not appearing as a lackey of the grouse-moor owners in Cleveland or a do-gooding rambler in North Yorkshire. After some initial setbacks, I developed a careful balancing act. I felt it equally important to attain a constructive dialogue with both the rural communities of the Park and the urban users and young people in Teesside and further afield. This dialogue between town and country came naturally to me with my planning background and brought immense satisfaction.

It is a great pity that this vital aspect of the National Parks was shamefully neglected until very recently and, even then, it took the influence of the voluntary sector led by the Council (now the 'Campaign') for National Parks to get some positive action through their Mosaic Programme. The efforts of the Park Authorities have been almost entirely focussed on the problems of the rural communities. While this is understandable, since good relations with the Parks' residents is essential, we live in a crowded island and the rural/urban divide is not narrowed by concentrating exclusively on one side of the division.

Fighting for Moorland

The divide was at the time most clearly revealed in our relationship with the farming community. In order to break down the 'them and us' attitude and develop a meaningful dialogue, a consultative committee was formed and regular meetings were held with owners and land agents, the latter proving particularly useful. The problem was not one of our own making; government had given free reign, and seemingly unlimited funds, to the Ministry of Agriculture to expand food production by intensive farming methods. We were there, along with other agencies, to try to mitigate the worst effects of this process.

By far the most pressing issue was the ploughing of moorland for improved grazing, or even arable farming, then a profitable operation given the subsidies and technology available. A significant breakthrough came with a Voluntary Notification Scheme with the Country Landowners' Association, which, although it did little to prevent ploughing in the short term and was a long way from solving the problem, was at least a recognition on the part of the farming community that there was indeed an environmental problem at all. Up to this time, 'reclaiming' the moor was viewed as an ideal way of increasing production and farm income, whereas now there was conservation of landscape and wildlife habitats to take into account.

This change in policy had come about largely because of the Porchester Report into the controversy over the ploughing of moorland on Exmoor, which had, in fact, recommended a stop to the process. Nevertheless, I considered it necessary to develop a defensive strategy aimed at conserving the 'core' moorland in the central ridges and plateaux of the Park, while adopting a less preservationist stance on the fringes of the moor. This seems like heresy now and, indeed, it was a policy that would land us in deep trouble later on. At the time, however, given the government policy on agriculture and the lack of financial resources to prevent ploughing, it appeared to be the only realistic approach to adopt.

Despite the weakness in the strategy, this informal zoning of the Park was the precursor to the Conservation Maps, which it subsequently became a duty of the Park Authorities to prepare.

Turning of the Tide

A major victory for conservation was won in a different context when the government decided to refuse planning permission on environmental grounds for the extraction of potash in the Whitby area after a long public inquiry in 1979. This was a highly significant U-turn on the government's part, as planning permission for the two mines at Whitby and Hawsker Bottoms had been granted only five years previously and it was the renewal of the permissions that was in question, not completely new projects.

I had managed to survive a very difficult period when the County Council, with its chairman sitting on the Park Committee, had tried to prevent the Park Committee from refusing renewal of the two planning applications. I can well remember the gasps of surprise from my own staff when I announced I would be recommending refusal and I am sure they felt I had taken on too much. It was indeed a testing time and every lever was used to try to persuade the Park Committee to renew the consents. When this failed, as it happened by a comfortable majority, since most members were appalled at the prospect of ruining the Heritage Coast with two more mining complexes, the County Council took the unprecedented step of exercising their right to withdraw the powers of the Park Committee to determine planning applications that straddled the park boundaries, as most large-scale mining proposals invariably did.

This came too late for the Whitby proposals and thus I attended a public inquiry to defend the Park Committee's decisions against the mining with

Boulby Potash Mine (Mike Kipling)

the County Council, my employers, on the opposite side of the table. With hindsight, a high-risk strategy but one which seemed perfectly right at the time. In fairness, it did not lead to any long-term souring of relations but I cannot help but feel that the seeds of independence for the National Parks were liberally sown at that time. Not for the first time in these controversial situations, I was grateful to some senior members of the Council who took a broad view of the applications and were prepared to make a stand to oppose the additional mines.

Trouble at Mill

The interpretation of the relationship between the Park Committee and the County Councils was inevitably a most sensitive subject and one not helped by the woolly nature of the legislation based on the unholy alliance. It proved possible for lawyers to reach different conclusions on some matters and was the cause of much unnecessary and wasted time and energy spent on deciding who did what.

Early in their new form after the 1974 reorganisation, the Dales Park Committee members decided they had had enough of County interference, as they saw it, and made what came to be known as a 'Unilateral Declaration of Independence' or UDI for short. The rationale for this process was based on the political upheaval in the former Northern Rhodesia, where a group of white settlers decided to go it alone.

There then occurred one of the more bizarre episodes in the long-running saga of the struggle for control of the Parks.

The arguments in the Dales, and elsewhere, reached such a level that a Select Committee of the House of Commons was obliged to examine the dispute in a special session. In the middle of a rail strike in 1976, we were all invited down to London to discuss the issues with MPs. The very way in which the various delegations were invited and presented struck me as distinctly odd. The Dales Committee, our sister committee and, like us, a committee of the same County Council and subject to the same rules and regulations, was separately invited and represented, whereas the Moors Committee, represented by the Chairman and me, appeared as part of the County Council delegation.

The discussions were amiable enough but never really got to grips with the niceties of the power struggle which was cropping up in several County-run parks. The Peak and Lake District Parks had managed to retain their independence after 1974 and so we had two classes of Parks that were reflected in the wide differences in expenditure between them. At one stage, one half of the total central government grant went to these two Parks. I gained the impression in the Select Committee that the MPs were surprised and dismayed, somewhat justifiably I feel, to learn of such deep divisions in the running of the National Parks.

Paying for Conservation – Responsibility without Power

Back on the Moors, the erosion of moorland continued in a most awesome form in the huge fires of the hot, dry summer of 1976. Large areas of peat

▲
Moorland Fire in 1976 (NPA)

were destroyed, some down to the base rock, creating desert-like
conditions. It was a dreadful scene but it did give us the opportunity to
experiment with new techniques of restoration. A research programme of
restoration using the resources of several University Departments and co-
ordinated by Roy Brown in the Park Office was drawn up and a number of
interesting projects were got underway. It led naturally to a more ambitious
programme of moorland management and eventually to a large-scale
moorland regeneration scheme. Some years later, I recall being surprised
that even trees could be established on some of the highest and most
burned-out sites, a reflection of the artificial state of our moorland
environment.

An integral part of the programme was a large-scale project to control
the spread of bracken. This proved very popular with the owners and
tenants of the moor and has since spawned much research and experiment
with considerable expenditure on chemical spraying. I confess to having
doubts about the efficacy of this treatment, particularly in the long term.

▲
Bracken Invasion of Moorland (NPA)

Not only does the bracken quickly return without follow-up treatments but its very existence is an indication of richer soils where woodland, not heather, is the natural cover.

The bracken-control project signalled an alternative approach to land use and management that was slowly becoming fashionable: a voluntary system fuelled by financial or other incentives that culminated in the 1981 Wildlife and Countryside Act. Since it had proved impossible, for one reason or another, to bring in controls over such matters as the ploughing of moorland and the drainage of wetlands, activities outside the scope of the Planning system, the concept of the management agreement was developed, initially by the Countryside Commission, as an alternative. This was a genuine attempt to obtain conservation by agreement and to plug a widening gap in the public control of land-use change, one which I had attempted in Farndale in the 1960s.

However, the 'management agreement' was, and is, a euphemism for more agricultural subsidy but usually with environmental rather than agricultural objectives. It was eagerly taken up by the Country Landowners' Association and the National Farmers' Union who viewed it as an attractive alternative to statutory controls. It was not compulsory, it provided for additional income or compensation and, in some circumstances, for income without any significant expenditure on the part of the farmer. It was no surprise, therefore, that some sceptics labelled it as a modern form of 'Danegeld'. It continues to form the basis of the European Agricultural Policy.

At the time, we were highly nervous about this seemingly bottomless pit of expenditure and the obvious scope for abuse. It appeared that any owner of a valuable habitat could devise a scheme for agricultural 'improvement' and we would be left with no alternative but to offer compensation to prevent it, whether it was truly intended or not. Difficult cases later emerged where the destruction of valuable limestone grassland and coastal heath could only be prevented by such payment. The government, having enthusiastically set up the scheme, gave us no money to administer it and we could not possibly compete with the agricultural subsidy system.

The question of public interest in private land management has never been satisfactorily resolved and represents to me a failure on the part of successive governments to face up to the problem. Had the same attitude been taken when planning controls were introduced in the 1940s and 1950s, I dread to think of the implications for the public purse and for the environment. Instead, the politicians of the time rightly insisted on a 'refusal without compensation' ethic, which has served the country well.

I could not see any good reason then why the agricultural grants and subsidies should not be conditional on environmentally-friendly farming on all our farms. If this nettle had been grasped by our politicians, we would not only have prevented the widespread destruction of habitats such as hedges, stone walls and wetlands throughout the country, but would, in so doing, have saved large amounts of public expenditure on subsidies, grants and management agreements. A generation of farmers would by now have grown up with a more sustainable form of management on their farms than the present intensive production system, and problems of surpluses would not have been so acute.

It remains a complete mystery to me why our politicians have been so weak, even naïve, in this area of government and they must bear a large portion of blame for the deterioration in our native environment.

Recreation in the Park

On a more positive note, our agendas in the 1970s were full of projects and schemes for visitors to enjoy the Park, though the scale of visitor penetration was causing many problems. Traffic volumes had increased substantially and congestion, albeit of a transient nature, was a serious problem in such 'honeypot' locations as Hutton-le-Hole and Thornton-le-Dale. A particular bête noire of the local community was the famous Lyke Wake Walk. This 42-mile long challenge walk had grown in popularity at an alarming pace and was giving rise to erosion along the route and support parties gathering in large numbers at remote places.

At most meetings with farmers and landowners and other local groups, doomsday forecasts of thousands of feet trampling the moors to death were frequently trotted out though, ironically, the walk was initiated by a local farmer. I was urged to do something to alleviate the impact and prevent other walks from developing. Much time was spent by both officers and members of the Park Committee at working parties to combat the growing menace, as it was commonly viewed, of the popularity of walking over the moors.

My heart was never really in this. Although there was undoubtedly some erosion of peat and other problems, the damage, both temporary and permanent, by the 20,000 or so brave souls who attempted the 42-mile 'crossing' of the moors each year was miniscule compared with the damage to the landscape by modern farming methods, to say nothing of the moor burning for grouse management which sometimes got out of control.

The physical impact of recreation on the Park, though at times a source of local annoyance, has never been great in total. It was intellectually dishonest to exaggerate the scale of the problem, I thought on one September evening as I travelled down Sutton Bank with the Vale of York ablaze from end to end with stubble burning.

'Going to war with the land' was how a friend described the new farming techniques as we watched a huge machine clearing away heather one day. Later, in the 1980s, we all struggled to find acceptable ways of combining new farming methods with the conservation of landscape and wildlife, a struggle still far from over.

Before the Beeching Plan and the closures which followed, the Park and surrounding area had a good network of railways. During the 1960s, most of them closed and presented both problems and opportunities to the Park Committee and local authorities for alternative uses such as footpaths and bridleways.

One of the first to close was the Helmsley to Scarborough line, which ran along the edge of the Vale of Pickering, bypassing the towns and villages strung along the main road, the A170. I argued for public ownership of the line to be retained as it would have made an excellent route for a road bypass, relieving the busy and winding main road. At the time, it was judged that traffic volumes, other than occasional peak flows during holiday periods, would not justify the expenditure, even though I maintained that it would make an excellent recreational route until such time as it was needed. These propositions came to nought and the line was sold off and disappeared in many places.

Another line that I sought to retain as a recreational route, from Scarborough to Whitby, had a more successful outcome as it was eventually purchased by the Scarborough Borough Council and opened up as a bridlepath. I was disappointed that the National Park Committee had not been able to find the necessary funds but the sale came at a time when there were a great many calls on our small budget. All credit though to the Borough Council who took the initiative and created a splendid recreational facility.

The Pickering to Whitby line, which was closed in 1965, passed through some of the most dramatic scenery in the Park, including the famous Newtondale Gorge. It was not long before a group of enthusiastic volunteers sought to reopen the line as a historic railway featuring steam engines. They worked extremely hard and were able to open a small section in the middle section of the line. I sought to persuade them to extend their operation to the whole of the line from Pickering to Grosmont, where it joined the still-operational Esk Valley Line. This extension, from 6 to 18 miles, stretched their resources to the limit and was only made possible by considerable financial help, including the purchase of much of the track by the Park Committee, through the County Council.

In the difficult task of persuading the Railway Trust to chance their arm and expand, I was helped considerably by the Chief Executive of the Countryside Commission, Reg Hookway. Although it gave the Trust several anxious years, it has proved a long-term blessing to have a readily accessible

▲
Lyke Wake Walk – Erosion at Hamer (NPA)
Lyke Wake Walk – Support Team, near Shunner How (NPA)
▼

Steam Train in Newtondale – The North Yorkshire Moors Railway (Mike Kipling)

terminus, rather than, as one observer at the time put it, 'going from nowhere to nowhere'. Despite several years of negotiation, I was unable to achieve the objective of running trains, particularly steam, through to Whitby but this has now been realised and the line is one of the most used and successful historic railways in Britain.

The end of the decade brought political changes that were to have far-reaching effects on land-use planning and management. It had been an action-packed era in the National Parks. Problems, conflicts and conservation battles were there in abundance and yet much had been achieved. For the first time, the North York Moors had a tailor-made statutory body to protect its landscape and wildlife, and to promote its enjoyment, served by a professional staff with increasing expertise based in its own headquarters in the Park. Programmes of work were in hand for a wide range of visitor facilities and the embryonic schemes of land management were providing good results and value for money.

Chapter 4
Pride and Prejudice
1979‒94

THE NATIONAL PARKS went through a turbulent and nerve-racking period during the 1980s. By the end of the 1970s, the Parks were well established with rapidly growing programmes of work for both conservation and recreation. The storm clouds of financial shortages had already begun to gather, however, and with the sharp change in political philosophy after the general election of 1979, our budgets were a constant source of worry. Cuts and yet more cuts were the order of the day but, despite the general decline in public services, in the Moors we managed to hold together a respectable programme of positive schemes as well as maintain our planning and other legal commitments.

Parks and Monetarism

Not that the attentions of our new political masters were confined to budget cuts. For the first time, serious proposals were made about raising income from sources other than the taxes and the rates. Sacred cows such as free car parks and free entry to visitor centres were questioned and some fierce debates took place about the issues involved in charging directly for services. Some saw this trend as a negation of National Park principles of making a beautiful landscape available to all. Others saw it as a means of bringing income into local communities and businesses. The debate was intensified by the introduction of fees for processing planning applications and charging for hitherto free services such as diverting public rights of way.

I was particularly worried about charging for planning applications. The planning process was unpopular as it was with local people, and the prospect of charging while refusing planning consent for local housing and other projects which did not meet our increasingly stringent requirements, was frightening to say the least. However, after some initial teething troubles, such worries were swept away in the general enthusiasm to privatise public services and activities. This affected us in due course in such matters as car park and property maintenance and even the provision of professional services, which, in local government, had traditionally been 'in house'.

It is salutary to recall a comment by a colleague at the time who remarked that such issues as the public versus private divide come around in cycles. In 2010, as I rewrite these notes, we are, once again, beginning to question the unbridled pursuit of profit and its impact on our public services.

As these changes were accompanied by spiralling unemployment, the effects on staff and members was profound. From a situation where a minimum amount of time and resources had been spent on budgeting, we became preoccupied with constant reviews and appraisals aimed at squeezing more juice out of the lemon. The whole emphasis and direction of our work was visibly changing as we became slaves on the altar of cash flow.

I did my best to restrict staff involvement to a minimum so that the work on the ground in the Park did not suffer over much. In practice, this meant spending a good deal of time at County Hall rather than in the Park, which was regrettable but was undoubtedly a more efficient use of the resources.

Danegeld

Finance also dictated in large measure the ability of the National Park Committee to conserve and protect the landscape of the Park. The Wildlife and Countryside Act of 1981 introduced a system of sticks and carrots, mainly the latter, for farmers based on a voluntary approach to conservation. Instead of widening controls over such matters as the ploughing of moorland and old pasture, or the removal of stone walls and hedges, the government opted for financial inducements. Thus, if the Park Authority wished to amend a farm improvement scheme in order to conserve important habitats or prevent visual damage to the landscape, it had to attempt to persuade the farmer or owner to enter into a management agreement and pay him handsomely for it on the dubious basis of 'profit foregone'.

Despite this inducement, many farmers chose to go ahead with their schemes, even if it meant forgoing substantial grants from the Ministry of Agriculture (MAFF). It was at times difficult to understand this but I think it boiled down to the prevailing culture of mistrusting all forms of bureaucracy, not forgetting that it was also usually profitable to carry out the works without grant aid.

There was a right of appeal to the MAFF if agreement with the Park could not be reached. This happened at Coxwold where a farmer wanted to plough up some ancient pasture of considerable conservation value. Eventually, he got tired of the delay and proceeded with his ploughing. There then followed an extraordinary, prolonged bureaucratic process involving the MAFF, the Department of the Environment and other government agencies to decide whether he should receive the 'improvement' grant retrospectively. Since, in those days, MAFF grants were confidential and individual awards were not publicly available, we were not to learn of the outcome. The environmental damage had, of course, been done.

An even more difficult case was Troutsdale Moor. This unmanaged stretch of heather, surrounded by forestry, was rapidly regenerating with birch and pine, and a local tenant farmer applied for a MAFF grant to convert it into improved pasture. After much deliberation, the Park Committee decided not to object on the basis that it was an isolated area of moor, detached from the main moorland areas, not readily visible from the surrounding roads and footpaths and with no particular known conservation value. The agricultural case, involving the retention of a young family, was also strong. This decision was in accordance with the policy of protecting the core moorland while taking a more flexible attitude on the fringes.

The decision provoked a storm of protest from the Yorkshire Wildlife Trust who mounted an effective campaign to try to reverse the Committee's decision. At one stage, the Committee Chairman and I were invited to a meeting with the protestors, which we held in the Chairman's house near York, where we had the objections read out to us, lawyer fashion, as we sat in his lounge. It was a most uncomfortable, if somewhat extraordinary, experience.

The campaign against the scheme continued and rare species and important eco-systems were suddenly and miraculously discovered as ecologists from far and wide descended on the moor because of the publicity. Eventually, the absentee landlords came to the rescue and forced abandonment of the whole project. Ironically, since that time and with little management, the moor has continued to rewild with the spread of mainly native trees and shrubs, and will soon be woodland rather than heath.

In retrospect, Troutsdale Moor, this unremarkable and virtually unknown stretch of heath, marked a turning point in the history of conservation in the Moors. From that time on, the Park Committee would have to take a strong line on improvement schemes regardless of cost or official policy. Compromise, ordinarily an essential ingredient of land management, was to be sidelined if the reputation and integrity of the Park Committee as a conservation agency was to be retained. The 'core moorland' policy would have to be jettisoned.

It was a severe lesson to me in realpolitik. That we were placed in this position was, of course, mainly due to the threat of large-scale compensation if we objected to schemes and, in turn, this was because of the absence of statutory controls in the Wildlife Act. The sticks simply did not work, only the carrots.

If You Can't Beat 'Em...

The unworkable system of the Act served to reinforce a long-held view of mine: that on critical sites it was often in the long-term public interest for the Park Authority to acquire the land and manage it directly for conservation and public access and enjoyment. We had already purchased the Hole of Horcum and Levisham Moor; nearby Nab Farm and Lockton High Moor were shortly to follow and, later, the Roman Camps on Cawthorn Moor.

I pushed these purchases through the system using every argument I could muster and with strong support from the Countryside Commission.

Coastal Scene at Port Mulgrave (NPA)

Later in the 1980s, I had to bow to the inevitable political realities, otherwise by now the Park Authority would probably own a greater range of sites and habitats in the Park. The Lockton High Moor case was particularly interesting in that I was able to demonstrate that purchase was a much more cost-effective solution to protecting the moor than an expensive management agreement, which, in any event, was of dubious long-term value. Another area I thought should be acquired was Carlton Bank where there were severe erosion problems linked to motorbike scrambling. This problem was resolved later and much money was spent on revegetating and landscaping the derelict areas.

An alternative solution to the virtual embargo on land purchase was to assist another like-minded body to step in. This happened at Port Mulgrave where a farmer proposed to reclaim an area of valuable coastal heath. A management agreement there would have been very expensive. After much discussion, during which the NFU proved particularly obdurate, I was instrumental in helping the National Trust to acquire the land under their Enterprise Neptune programme. It is an interesting reflection that purchase by the National Trust, itself a quasi-public body, was viewed as perfectly acceptable whereas purchase by the Park Authority was seen as land nationalisation. These nuances of political philosophy, though extremely frustrating to those of us trying to protect the moor, had to be acknowledged if progress was to be made.

The links with the National Trust were good and regular meetings were held with their staff to our mutual benefit. I remember being asked by the Council for National Parks to assist their new manager in demonstrating the workings of the planning system and other aspects of countryside work. That raw recruit, a charming young lady, was Fiona Reynolds, now Dame Fiona and the Director General of the National Trust.

Fencing

The ploughing of the moor became a less attractive proposition to farmers during the late 1980s. Apart from falling returns in the market, the grant system was gradually refined to discourage such 'improvements', and pressure from the conservation agencies and public opinion served to emphasise this. Fencing the open moor remained an issue, however, especially with increased traffic on the roads and the problem of sheep deaths.

I have always had an inherent dislike of fencing on the moor. It destroys the wonderful feeling of freedom and open space, which is one of the chief aesthetic assets of the Park. Many subscribe to the same view but farmers find it difficult to understand with their senses attuned to the problems of managing sheep. Thus proposals to fence off the main roads over the moor, which increasingly cropped up, inevitably became controversial. I admired the strong stance taken by the Countryside Commission at this time; they fully appreciated the wider impact of fencing, sadly, unlike some of the local Park Committee members who, increasingly during this period, were narrowing the vision of what the National Park was all about.

After the usual long debates and negotiations, a policy was evolved to permit the fencing of the A-class roads only, though the pressures remained for fencing on some of the other well used roads such as the Hutton-le-Hole to Castleton road over Blakey Rigg. The problem of sheep deaths has proved a most intractable one and various attempts are still being made to deal with it, the latest involving the erection of warning signs with solar panels which, unfortunately, are in themselves quite intrusive. Tourists got the blame in the 1980s but, as many sheep are killed at night or early in the morning, it appeared that local people were also involved.

Farm Conservation – the Holy Grail

The fencing proposals posed the classic dilemma to the Park Committee: how to square the economic interests of a small, though important, section of the population with the wider purposes of the National Park. The solution, increasingly, was to throw money at the problem by way of management agreements. The difficulty with this strategy was that it ignored, even inflamed, the economic pressures to increase production through the Community Agricultural Policy (CAP), in this case to graze more sheep. Or, as one of our Committee members put it, 'the Danes keep a coming'.

Combining the two systems, the agricultural and environmental in a sustainable way, was the obvious way to overcome this dilemma. This we began to try to do in the Moors in sheer desperation at the lack of initiative on the part of the government, who, amazingly, considering the prevailing monetarist policies, seemed quite content, apart from a little sniping from time to time, to continue the heavy and often unnecessary expenditure on grants and subsidies under the umbrella of the CAP. One of the government's environment ministers of the time called the CAP 'the engine of destruction', yet the subsidies continued to flow, and still do, though with greater environmental safeguards.

The individual farmer could not be blamed in this situation. He was encouraged by the CAP and his peers to grow as much food as possible, despite the growing surpluses, though many were unhappy with the impact of modern methods.

We decided to get behind our own farmers to see what could be achieved locally.

The first pioneering effort was a scheme for Farm Conservation Plans. This was a simple survey of a candidate farm to first identify small-scale conservation projects which would enhance the landscape and wildlife

Launch of the Farm Scheme by David Curry,
MP, left, with Park Chairman, George Sigsworth
and the Author, Farndale, 1990 (NPA)

habitats and then to fund the most promising; examples included tree and hedge planting, pond creation and rebuilding stone walls.

The next step, which was much more ambitious, was to devise a whole farm conservation plan which went beyond the somewhat cosmetic attempts of the first plans to integrate the actual day-to-day management of the farm with approved conservation methods. Six pilot schemes were set up with management payments being made on an annual basis for implementing the plans. The grants were integrated with the CAP grants as far as possible, even using them to secure some improvements. The annual payments under the scheme began to account for a substantial part of the farm income and later, when the scheme was further refined and extended, represented a long-term future for hill sheep farming based on sound ecological principles.

Although there had been a few attempts to conserve valuable habitats by way of management agreements, the Grazing Scheme in the Broads for the Halvergate Marshes being one of the first such experiments, no one to my knowledge had attempted to plan for the management of the whole farm for conservation purposes.

The net result, though short of a truly environmentally orientated system of all farm grants and subsidies, was that large and continuous areas of the inner dales of the Park were being managed in accordance with Park policies and the farmers were being rewarded for so doing. So successful was the 'Farm Scheme', as it was simply called, that the vast majority of farmers in the selected dales chose to join in and the scheme attracted considerable national publicity. As a result, I was invited in 1993 to explain the scheme to an international audience at a conference in America which had been set up to explore the mechanisms and feasibility of utilising local communities to run conservation schemes, mainly in the third world.

I was given pride of place at a meal with the US Secretary of State for the Interior but found him somewhat hostile to the idea of subsidising farmers for environmental purposes. He, in certain respects quite rightly, was deeply suspicious of the CAP and gave me the impression that the US did not want to go down this 'European route', though I later learned that a similar approach to our scheme was being adopted to deal with a problem of forest grazing lands in Oregon and, of course, the Americans were also busily protecting their farmers in other ways.

Every management scheme, however successful, has its downside and I am convinced that an unfortunate side effect of the success of the Farm Scheme was that the Moors Park was excluded from areas selected nationally to receive additional funding for environmentally sensitive farming, the so-called ESAs. It was, perhaps, no coincidence that we received somewhat generous grant settlements for our budget at this time as a form of compensation. We also had the satisfaction that the National Park, rather than a central government department or agency, was running a scheme which had important and valuable implications for the local communities in the Park.

Extending the Tarmac

One particularly irksome issue rumbled on in the Moors. It is an innate tendency for road engineers to want constantly to improve and upgrade all the roads under their control and, indeed, they are often under considerable local pressure to do so. Over the years, despite the expressed opposition of the Park Committee, many tracks over the moors had been tarmacked and widened thus opening up remote stretches of the Park to the motor vehicle and degrading the qualities of quietness and solitude for which the Park was designated.

A scheme to surface part of the Stape to Egton Bridge road, which had never been properly surfaced, deserved the condemnation of the Park Committee but it was powerless to prevent it proceeding. It was one more classic example of the lack of teeth of a National Park Authority faced with an undesirable project by a different arm of the public service. Another controversial scheme was a straightening of the sharp bends at Ellerbeck on the A169, Whitby to Pickering main road. This would have resulted in a spare area of land, which might have served as a picnic area. Fortunately, the scheme was the victim of budget cuts and has not materialised.

There was a gradual hardening of attitude in the late 1980s and early 1990s towards road widening and improvement in sensitive areas like the National Parks. It became evident that if the qualities of quietness and solitude were ever to be enjoyed in the Parks, the motor car should not dominate the scene. This was shown in a very direct and graphic way in the Yorkshire Dales where the County Council was asked, and eventually agreed, to retain the main road through Wensleydale largely in its present form and not seek to upgrade it.

In the Moors, the most controversial road scheme, apart from several ideas to improve the notorious steep Sutton Bank, was the widening of the road through Hutton-le-Hole. This early scheme had been the subject of much consultation involving not only the Park Authority but also the, then new, Countryside Commission. Our highway colleagues had attended to the matter with the most painstaking attention to detail and I felt they had done a splendid job, though we all regretted the loss of the old ford or 'water splash'. I was, however, somewhat deflated when I showed the results to the Commission members whose reaction was that, while the landscaping and detailing were of a high standard, we had 'Surreyfied' the village scene. Difficult to win that one!

Education and the Media

One of the great advances during the 1980s was in the field of environmental information and interpretation. From hesitant beginnings with displays and exhibitions in our visitor centres in the 1970s, we set about a policy of constant improvement and innovation, not only in the centres but in the provision of publications and services to school and youth organisations.

The methods became ever more sophisticated and refined. It is impossible to quantify the value of these ongoing activities, though the consistently high placing we achieved in national surveys indicated that the standards were high. It seemed to me that the face to face work amongst schools and youth bodies was particularly valuable and rewarding, made all the more so by good support and liaison with the two County Council education departments.

Apart from the provision of information and interpretation services, which all National Parks were and are required to do by law, the staff were devoting more

▲
Meeting Princess Diana
at Chatsworth, 1987 (NPA)

time and effort to general PR work with the local and national media. This commitment grew gradually over the years until I began to wonder if it might take over our working lives altogether. To the best of my knowledge, no National Park Authority had the courage to appoint a professional PR officer, such commercial-sounding appointments being frowned upon in the public service arena, though I did feel it would be cost-effective, if only to deflect some of the pressure in time and energy from the senior staff.

Many people in public life tend to be critical of the media. I have to say that, apart from the odd inaccurate news item, I found the vast majority of reporters and interviewers to be professional and keen to present a fair account of the issues. My experience with the local newspapers was on the whole a pleasurable one. Not only did they report regularly on the range of National Park work, they also did much to call into question some of the more extreme statements put out by aggrieved individuals.

Some of the interviews stand clear in my memory: squatting in the heather with a presenter on a BBC Radio interview to reveal suddenly the surreal spectacle of the Fylingdales Early Warning Station to the listener; having to repeat an introduction to a BBC TV interview on moorland ploughing about a dozen times because of my inability to stop walking at the precise moment; spending a most enjoyable half hour with Princess Diana at Chatsworth; having lunch with the Queen and the Duke of Edinburgh at Pickering when I was accidentally presented as Mr Kellie from the Forestry Commission.

During the late 1980s, the BBC decided to make an in-depth documentary about the National Park. Their camera crew spent a whole year obtaining some splendid footage of the wildlife and other aspects of the Park. When the documentary entitled 'Land of Wild Freedom' was launched at a ceremony at the Moors Centre at Danby, it was announced that the film could hardly fail as the proceedings would be opened by Trueman and Statham! Freddie Trueman did the voice over.

The event which gave me most pleasure, however, was the publication of the definitive work on the landscape of the Moors, *The North York Moors*

Staff of the North York Moors, including the Whitby Nun, at Chatsworth, 1987 (NPA)
▼

Landscape Heritage, in which I had contributed the final chapter. The series editor for this splendidly researched work was Prof. Allan Patmore, a long-standing friend who has done such a marvellous job in supporting both the Park Authority and the Association. I was justly proud to succeed him as President.

Writing had long been a hobby of mine since my University days and during my time with the National Parks I had several opportunities to put my ideas into print, including a contribution to the British Association for the Advancement of Science and an essay in a book on Recreation and the Environment, published to commemorate Allan's retirement from academia. Later, after my own retirement, I was able to contribute two sections in the *Historical Atlas of North Yorkshire*, a millennium publication.

Maintaining Momentum

Staffing the National Park department during the 1980s was a contradictory process. There was no real shortage of money to appoint the small number needed but, because the County Council along with the rest of local government was cutting back most of the time, I was forced to comply with ultra-strict rules of recruitment, including very low salaries. This was offset by the rising unemployment so it was not too difficult to find suitable candidates.

The lack of employment opportunities had another effect: professional staff tended to stay for long periods. This was helpful in stabilising the staffing arrangements but meant that well-qualified and competent staff had few chances to further their experience, essential in environmental careers. I did my best to overcome this by moving people around as much as possible. One particularly fruitful example was the secondment of one of my deputies, Nick Pennington, to a UK government sponsored job in Barbados for a year, aimed at exploring the possible creation of a National Park there. This was made possible by the kind assistance of the Countryside Commission, who seconded one of their senior officers, Sally Bucknall, for the period. This made the national headlines as it was most unusual for a woman to be appointed to a post of this nature at the time, strange though this may seem today.

Another opportunity for gaining alternative experience occurred when the Council for National Parks (CNP) wanted a suitable person to take

▲

Cawthorn Camps, Manpower Service Commission Work Party (NPA)

charge of their staff for a short period. I was able to arrange for Val Dilcock, then a planner in development control, to take a secondment to London for six months. This strengthened our links with this important body.

These and other arrangements meant that not only did the staff concerned gain valuable alternative experience, but fresh ideas and thinking were introduced to their departments and I feel that everyone concerned benefited.

I was able to participate in an exchange arrangement whereby the Chief Executive of the Broads Authority took over my post for a short period while I did the same down in Norwich. I found this brief exchange immensely informative and stimulating, especially so because of the input by the Broads staff to my understanding of their work. One of this talented group, David Brewster, subsequently came to work with me in the Moors.

One of the lesser-known contributions to the Park during the 1980s was the work on practical management jobs carried out by the Manpower

Services Commission. For a time, the expenditure on contracts undertaken by these young teams from Teesside and Scarborough far outweighed the Park's budget. Their work programmes were not always very efficient but it was to everyone's advantage to have these youngsters working in the fresh air of the Park rather than kicking their heels on the streets of Middlesbrough. For many of them, it was the first experience of the countryside and it made an indelible impression on some. It was a thoroughly Keynsian solution to the problems of economic recession, regrettably abandoned when the economy improved, though revived again in the late 1990s, and quite likely about to re-emerge in some form in the current recession.

The Association is Born

In 1985, another event of long-term importance to the Park occurred: the creation of the North Yorkshire Moors Association (NYMA). For several years, I had been concerned about the weak and fragmented support for the Park from the voluntary sector. We had a hardworking and effective band of voluntary rangers, as they came to be called, but they could not get involved in the policies and politics of the Park. At the national level, the CNP kept an eye on major developments and made representation to government ministers and departments on Park policies.

What was lacking was a support body with similar aims to the CNP to act as a local, Park-level, watchdog. Groups representing the various economic interests in the Park were well established and organised, and this created an imbalance when major developments and policy issues were under discussion. Some of the other Parks had such support groups with some, such as the Friends of the Lake District, considerably predating the Park designation. The various branches of the Council for the Protection of Rural England in North Yorkshire and Cleveland did a valuable job but their interests were spread over wide areas outside the Park.

Fortunately there were at this time a number of people with a strong personal commitment to the protection of the Moors who were prepared to bring other, like-minded persons together. The three stalwarts who initially took up the challenge were Major Peter Walker, then a member of

▲
The 'Gang of Four' at the Launch of the Esk Valley Walk, 1992
Left to Right: Major Peter Walker, The Author, Gerald McGuire, Dr. Don Tilley (NPA)

Visit of Chris Bonnington, President of CNP, 1993 (NPA)
▼

the National Park Committee, Gerald McGuire, a well-known rambler and also a long-serving member of the Committee, and Dr. Don Tilley, a retired hospital consultant, who took on the onerous task of setting up the administrative machinery of the new Association. I helped to establish the group, we were dubbed 'the Gang of Four', but once established I could of course take no active part in the running of the Association, at least until I eventually retired.

The new Association inevitably took some time to become an effective voice in the Park and had to debate and decide on its title, logo and remit, but it was a great comfort to me to have its moral support and it certainly filled a gap in the range of bodies with interests in the National Park.

Tourism

A recurring theme during the 1980s was the development of tourism. Up until this time, tourism had been regarded as a supplementary economic activity to the other main employers, farming and mining, as the numerous Bed and Breakfast signs outside farmhouses in the Park indicated. Most local people regarded jobs in the tourist trade as 'soft' and temporary or even ephemeral and not really proper employment. By the end of the decade, it was apparent even to the most diehard, conservative local that tourism was rapidly overtaking the other activities as an employer and user of capital. There had been a veritable explosion of holiday cottages, for instance, and theme parks and other enterprises were springing up in and around the Park.

This posed difficult philosophical and political, as well as practical, problems which still have not been properly addressed. If the main economic value of the area is as a tourist resort, then why continue to subsidise, with large amounts of public funds, the farming and other land-using activities?

The standard reply is that we need the farmers to manage the landscape which the tourists enjoy and this, of course, is the current policy. Farmers have become Park keepers. I recall, with some irony, a conference on the future of the Parks held in Northumberland in the 1970s when an impassioned plea was made by a very articulate wife of a local hill farmer,

▲ Log Cabins, Keldy, Dalby Forest (NPA)　　　▲ B&B signs on the Coast (NPA)

Guided Walk at Horcum (Mike Kipling)
▼

that hill farmers had to be maintained otherwise they would become Park keepers, with all the humiliation that that implied. Again, this is an indication of just how much attitudes have changed.

The 'keep things as they are' policy is a strong one but ignores the very real benefits which might accrue from a change to a more diverse land-use policy with more woodland and wildlife reserves. This would release much needed public money for other purposes, including local housing, and assist with the problems arising from climate change and biodiversity.

Such changes, which are now being seriously examined, and will certainly come under the spotlight when the CAP is reviewed in 2013, seemed a long way off when I launched the Alternative Land Use Scheme in 1990. The idea was to experiment with new ways of managing marginal agricultural land, including 'rewilding' to diversify and enrich the landscape and wildlife of the Park, in effect to fulfil the often forgotten legal requirement to enhance the landscape, rather than merely to protect it, worthy though that is.

Thornton-le-Dale (Mike Kipling)
▼

New Stile near Roseberry Topping (NPA)
▼

Several small-scale projects were undertaken, including natural regeneration in felled conifer woodlands (now becoming standard practice) and restoration of calcareous grassland. The aim of taking marginal farmland out of production was only an idea at the time, as the subsidy system made any large-scale changes uneconomic. Since then, several large rewilding schemes have occurred, mostly by private landowners or voluntary bodies, sadly not by or in the National Parks. One such scheme, which we had agreed with all the interests concerned on a large area on the Hambleton Hills, fell through when the owner tired of waiting for the scheme to finalise. It would have involved the recreation of moorland and extension of woodland on previously arable land, temporarily in 'set aside'.

Rewilding at Bumble Wood, Wheeldale (NPA)
▼

Access for Recreation

Associated with the expansion of tourism was the ever-present issue of public access on foot in the National Parks. The solution on enclosed and farmed land was a well-maintained network of public rights of way and we worked steadily towards this objective throughout the 1980s and 1990s.

On the open moors, the issue of the right to roam, or 'open access', flared up from time to time. In the North York Moors, we had been lucky in inheriting a 'live and let live' attitude towards public access. We were sometimes criticised for a lack of access agreements but whenever I discussed the matter with the landowners, we both concluded that the 'de facto' access situation served all sides tolerably well; the landowners tolerated virtually unrestricted access, though reserved the right to step in if things got out of hand, and the Park Committee was saved the expense and commitment of bureaucratic management agreements. This type of 'gentlemen's agreement' worked well most of the time, only being spoilt by occasional vandalism on the part of some visitors and over-zealous restrictions on the part of a small minority of owners and gamekeepers.

Walkers on Moorland Track (NPA)
▼

It was, of course, no substitute for a legal right of access on the moors. The issue divided many sections of society, including the NYMA. I had always been in favour of a legal right, though I was not keen on Access Agreements. In my opinion, which I freely expressed, the grant of a legal right would make very little difference to the situation as the number of people wishing to track across heather away from rights of way was unlikely to alter. It would, however, make for peace of mind for the small number of folk who did wish to explore and, furthermore, make the legal situation absolutely clear in the event of conflict.

To me, the issue was one of principle or human rights, rather than a pressing management problem. Despite all the dire warnings, it is satisfying to see that the experience to date of the granting of the right in recent years has not led to any serious conflicts. The same will, I am sure, apply to the granting of access along the coast. In the Moors, we are fortunate in having a well-maintained national trail, the Cleveland Way, along the coast but, even so, there are problems when the route is eroded by cliff erosion and, in some places, the path is very restricted with fencing hard on the landward side. I have always argued that access on foot to the coast is of prime importance and a wide strip of land should be set aside for recreation.

The Fylingdales Saga

The Moors Park has been home to the UK's primary early warning station for nuclear missiles since 1962. The famous radomes, or 'golf balls', and associated structures were erected in a great hurry at that time, at the height of the Cold War, on Fylingdales Moor. Although the Park Committee was consulted, the extent of the consultation was minimal and the members were asked to treat the information in strict confidence. They were told, and the Ministry of Defence confirmed, that a site on the Moors was the only one to meet the very strict operational criteria.

The station employed a large number of staff, including local people who were bused out daily from Whitby and Pickering. It apparently played a major role in the country's defence for some 25 years, when its technology became dated and it was necessary to replace the mechanically operated radomes with electronic radar.

▲
RAF Fylingdales Early Warning Station, 1984 (NPA)
RAF Fylingdales, 1993, with the new Radar Station, just before
the removal of the 'Golf Balls' (NPA)
▼

At this stage, a discovery was made by the NYMA that the site in the Moors had in fact been a compromise between a site in Scotland, favoured by the Americans, who largely funded the station and its operation, and the British who wanted a site in East Anglia. The fact that it was in a National Park had clearly carried little weight. Now that a major redevelopment was proposed, involving the replacement of the radomes by a single large radar shaped like a truncated pyramid, I thought it necessary to revisit the claim that the site should be in the National Park.

The technical reasons for evaluating this were beyond our resources. The Committee was divided over the issue of retaining the station. In the circumstances, they adopted my recommendation that we should ask the Secretary of State for the Environment, who was responsible for protecting the Park and who, unlike the Park Committee, would have access to the confidential technical information, to satisfy himself that the defence needs of the country outweighed the strong environmental objections to retaining and redeveloping the site in a National Park.

I cannot claim that I was surprised at the result to go ahead but it at least put the responsibility firmly with the government. Thus visitors to the Park are faced with the site of this extremely ugly radar in many views in the centre of the Park. The same objection could be, and indeed was, levelled at the former 'golf balls', but one has to admit that, in a surreal way appropriate to the space age, they possessed a special quality that reflected the moorland environment in which they were sited. Their spherical shape and disposition flowed with the contours of the moor to create a unique scene.

Indeed, when the decision became known, there were those who felt that the golf balls should be retained as 'listed buildings', such was their contribution to the landscape. I can only hope that when the present radar is obsolete, a stronger stance is taken on removing the station from the National Park.

Research

Throughout my career, I had always taken a keen interest in research on land-use matters. This stems partly from my earlier academic experience but also from an innate wish to change the British countryside for the

▲
Affordable Local Housing, Egton (NPA)

better. Whenever the opportunity occurred and I could find time to set aside, I would put my ideas and experience in writing or join other groups to extend the boundaries of land-use planning and management.

Thus, I wrote from time to time in professional journals and contributed to books on the environment, did examination work for several universities and the Town Planning Institute and took an active part in professional groups such as the Association of National Park Officers, being their chairman in 1976 and again in 1990. For a time, I was a director of Tees Valley Tourism and sat on several other committees and groups over the years, including an EU committee on environmental law.

The job of National Park Officer provides many such opportunities for contact with a wide range of people and organisations and I shall always be grateful to the National Park Committee and the County Council for encouraging me to take on board what I felt I could reasonably cope with at any time.

This side of my career became especially important to me during the 1980s when, for a time, I began to wonder whether the Parks and the planning system would survive the onslaught of the radical changes to society involving privatisation and the dismantling of public services. For many years, critics of the planning system had chipped away at the unnecessary bureaucracy as they saw it, and for a time they found a sympathetic ear in government.

The nadir of land-use planning was reached in the middle of the decade when general planning policy was slackened to such an extent by one Secretary of State that there was a danger of the system collapsing under an 'anything goes' scenario. Fortunately, and perversely, the NIMBY attitude of the influential middle classes actually secured the survival of the system as, without it, their properties and land could not be protected from undesirable development.

Eventually, a U-turn in policy led to a new, 'plan led' system being introduced whereby development control decisions had to conform with the Local Plan produced by the District Planning Authorities generally, but by the NPAs in the Parks. I was initially suspicious of this change of emphasis as it put the Secretary of State in a very strong controlling position since the Local Plan had to conform with the Structure Plan prepared by the Counties which, in turn, needed the approval of the Secretary of State. It proved, however, a robust system and cut out some of the parochial decision making in some areas that was undermining the national policies.

Those who thought the NPA was being too restrictive with such matters as holiday cottage conversions or houses for locals in the villages had to argue their case against the framework of a plan with strong policies built into it detailing the criteria to be used. It had another unforeseen but beneficial effect: it made it more difficult for planning committee members to introduce local, personal issues into the decisions, which they had a habit of doing.

Independence

Government also changed tack, slowly, on another long-standing issue in the Parks. The question of the independence of the Park Authorities had simmered more or less continually since the Act of 1949 had fudged the issue. Gradually, for a number of reasons not all directly related to the running of the Parks, those favouring independence began to win the arguments. The process accelerated greatly after the visits of the Edwards Committee around the Parks. This Committee had been set up by government to examine the organisation and performance of the NPAs. I understand it was less than enamoured with some of the controls and administrative systems imposed by the County Councils.

I cannot help but feel, however, that the decision to make the Park Committees independent of local government owed as much to the general trend of hostility towards local government by central government that characterised the late 1980s and early 1990s. In the Moors we had fought, and in most cases won, the battles for more independence. The final act in this long-running saga had been an agreement reached during discussions at County Hall on the work of the Edwards Committee. A management scheme for the governance of the Park, which also applied to

Visit of the National Park Review Panel, the 'Edwards Committee', 1990 (NPA)
▼

▲

The Three NPOs of the North York Moors, 1974 to the Present
Left to Right: the Author, the Late David Arnold-Forster, Andy Wilson

the Yorkshire Dales, and which gave the Park Committees and the Park Officers virtual operational independence.

This system was working well at the time I retired and provided a useful run-in to legal independence, which later followed. Now, with a growing antagonism towards Quangos, which is basically what the current Park Authorities are, one wonders how long it will be before the control of the Parks comes back on the agenda. As a planner, I have tended to favour a regional approach to land-use planning but, unfortunately, regionalism is out of fashion and a vacuum is opening up between central and local government planning. In a crowded island, some planning at the regional level is not only sensible, it is essential to achieve the right balance between local and broader interests, especially when deciding on major developments.

For, despite my long experience in rural planning, I remain an unrepentant 'town and country' planner. This island is too small, too pressurised, to permit the segregation of its 60 million inhabitants into a large urban majority pursuing its life independently from a much smaller, rural minority. The National Parks have a vital role to play in this but they must relate to the needs of the urban population as well as the local residents. The recent designation of two new Parks in the crowded south of England should help to address this issue.

Epilogue

SINCE THESE NOTES WERE first put on paper in 1997, a great deal has happened in the National Park scene, much of it encouraging. The New Forest and the South Downs have at last achieved National Park status and two Parks have been created in Scotland with other candidates under consideration. All the Parks are independently run, though the age-old arguments about planning control have resulted in some odd arrangements which, hopefully, will be rationalised before long.

Not only have new Parks come into being but the status of the old ones has undoubtedly risen with a wide acceptance of their value across the political spectrum and in the public mind generally. In effect, they have become 'mainstream' in the public service. While this is an achievement to be welcomed, it has the danger of losing some of the pioneering spirit which characterised the period of my service.

There are a great many worthwhile projects and initiatives in the Parks at present, including some very well thought out ones in the Yorkshire Parks, but there are already signs that the bolder initiatives in environmental planning and management are being taken elsewhere, particularly by voluntary bodies such as the Royal Society for the Protection of Birds and the National Trust. If I were a young planner today, I would have to think seriously about joining one of these bodies for there is nothing more worthwhile and stimulating than extending the frontiers of our knowledge of the management of the environment.

The history of the British National Parks has, in many ways, centred on the tension between national and local interests. Obtaining the right balance is often difficult and elusive. My perception of recent work in the Parks is that the pendulum has swung towards the local interest and away from the broader vision of enhancing the landscapes we have inherited. Two important trends will probably rectify this balance. Firstly, the impact of climate change which, if the scientists are right, will mean fundamental changes in wildlife and biodiversity, necessitating bold management measures. Secondly, the seemingly inexorable rise in population. As the south of the country in particular becomes more and more crowded, so the value of the sparsely populated Parks will increase.

The devolution of powers to Wales and Scotland is another potential problem. Keeping the family of National Parks together was a widely accepted objective in my experience. If different systems of governance or policy are adopted, the Parks as a family will split apart and the concept inevitably will be weakened. There are warning signs too about the status and value of our Parks internationally where there are criticisms that biodiversity objectives are not strong enough and there is not enough emphasis on wildlife conservation.

The conclusion I draw is that there is and remains a great need for those of us who love the wildness of the Parks, in the CNP and the Park Societies, to make our voice heard in government, nationally and locally, and perhaps, even more importantly, in our schools and universities.